HAL LEONARD GUITAR REPERTOIRE
Book 1 · Elementary

JOURNEY THROUGH THE
CLASSICS

COMPILED AND EDITED BY JOHN HILL

Cover Art: Vasily Andreyevich Tropinin

ISBN 978-1-4803-5592-7

7777 W. BLUEMOUND RD. P.O. BOX 13819 MILWAUKEE, WI 53213

In Australia Contact:
Hal Leonard Australia Pty. Ltd.
4 Lentara Court
Cheltenham, Victoria, 3192 Australia
Email: ausadmin@halleonard.com.au

Visit Hal Leonard Online at
www.halleonard.com

The pieces in this collection are presented in an *approximate* progressive order of difficulty, with the understanding that what is easy for one player may present challenges for the next. Fingerings for the right and left hands have been added to assist the player in the correct approach to technique and performance. However, many passages have been left without fingerings, in part due to the repetitive nature of the music, and to allow the player and teacher to explore their own approach to the music. Tablature has been added as a reference to assist with sight-reading, although the player is encouraged to use the standard notation whenever possible. The music in this collection has enriched the lives of people for several centuries, so play and enjoy!

– John Hill

CONTENTS

Etude in A Minor

Anonymous

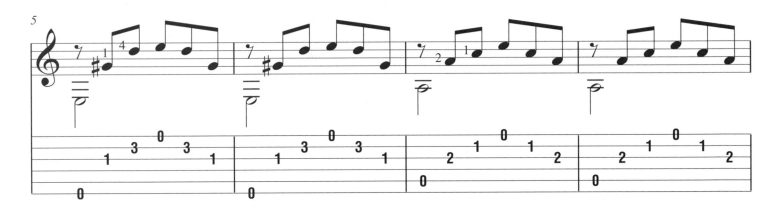

Study in D Minor

Anonymous

Moderato

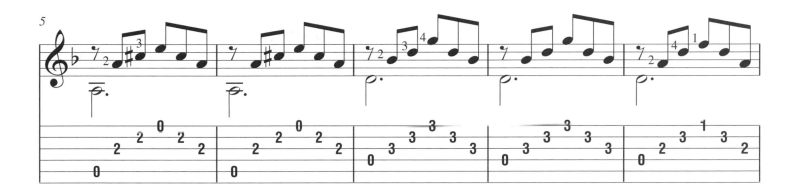

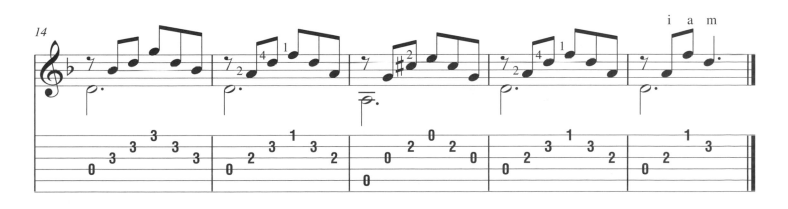

Romanza

Spanish Folk Song

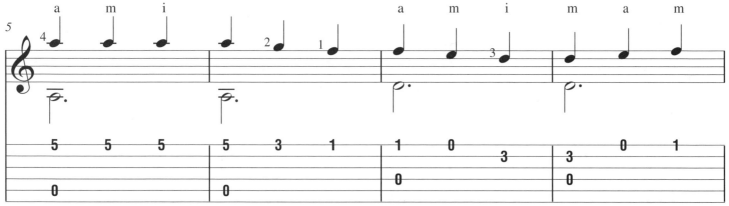

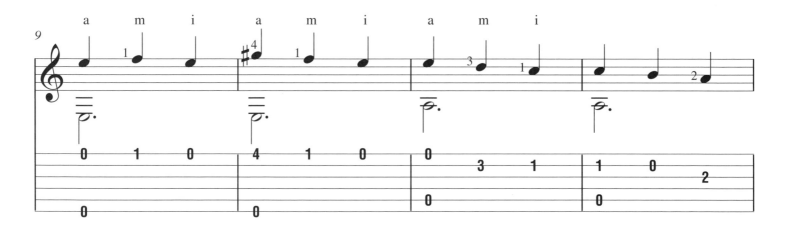

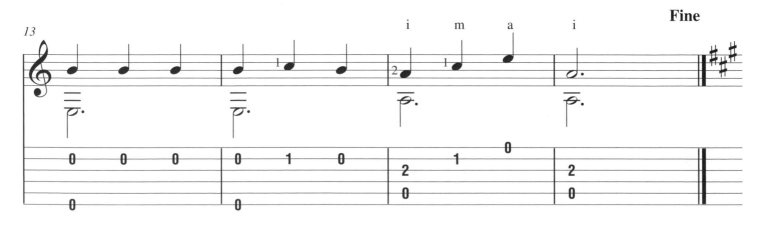

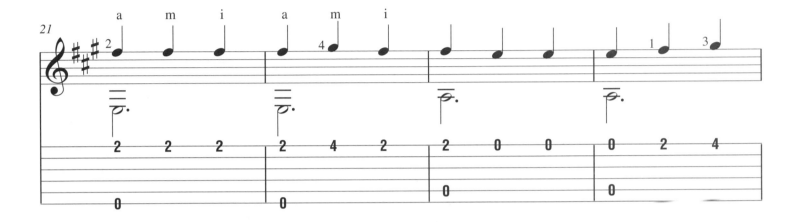

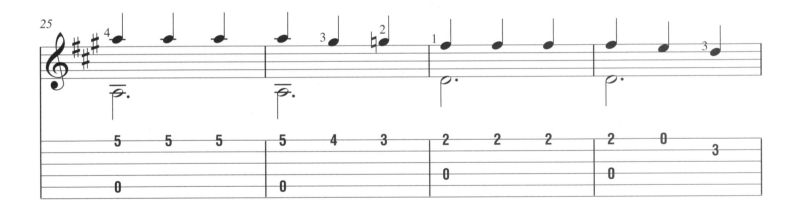

D.C. al Fine

Allegro, Op. 30

Mauro Giuliani
(1781-1829)

Allegro

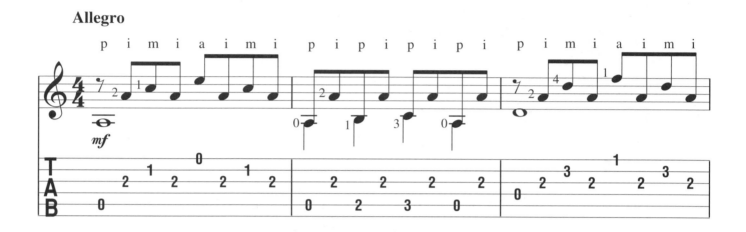

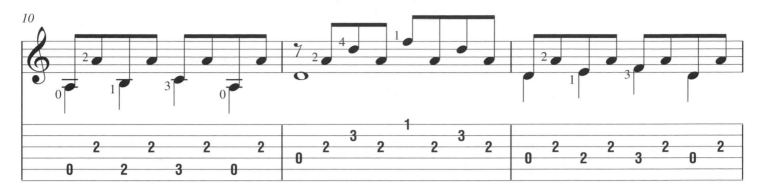

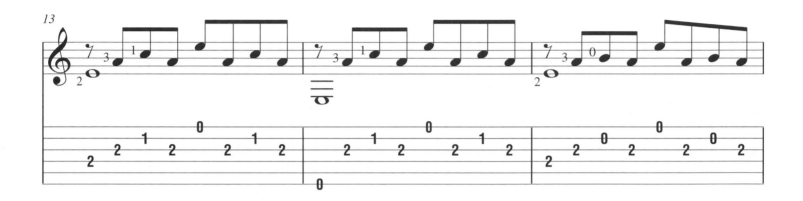

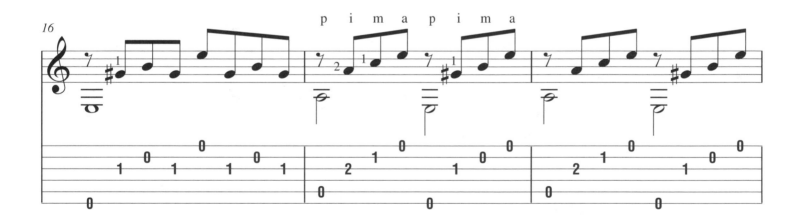

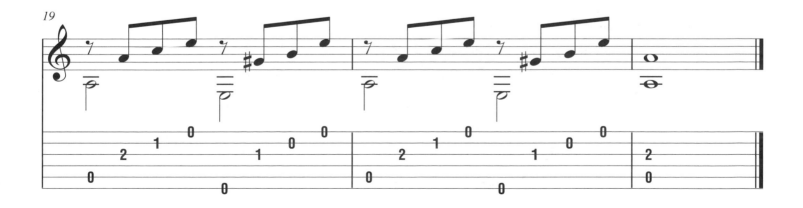

Spanish Dance

John Hill
(1953-   )

Moderato

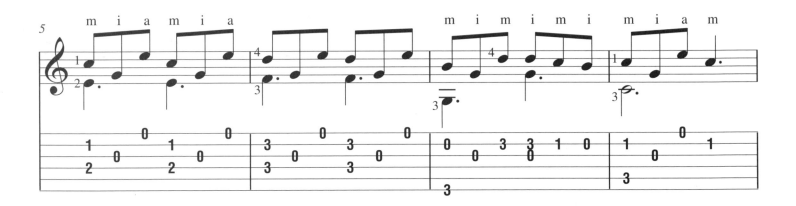

Miller's Dance

John Hill
(1953-   )

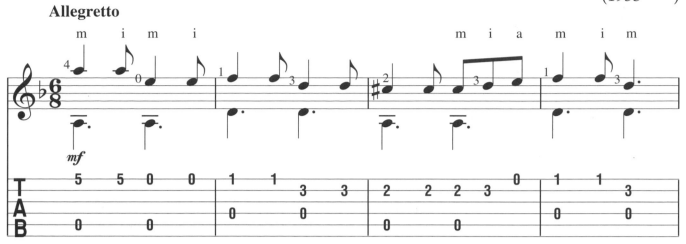

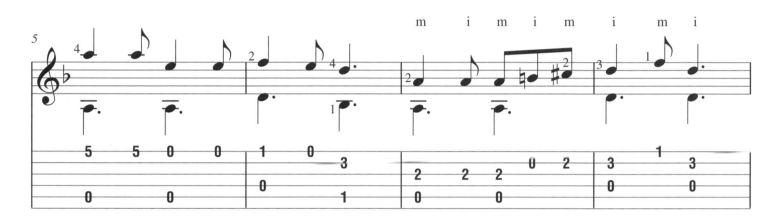

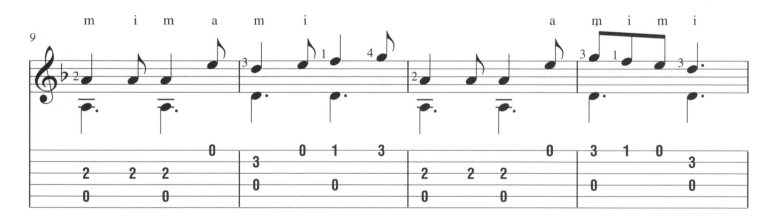

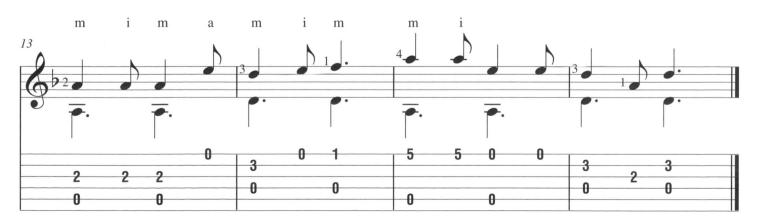

Menuett

Robert de Visée
(c.1660-c.1720)

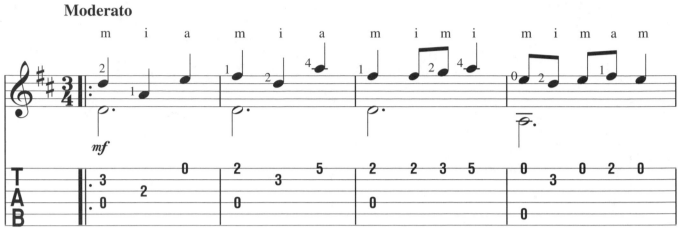

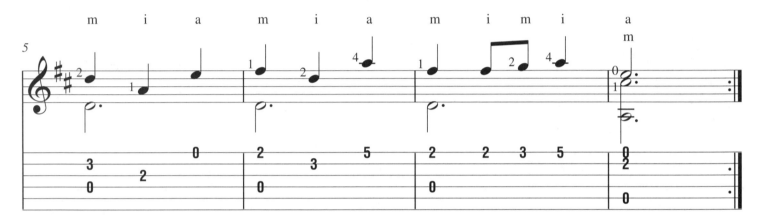

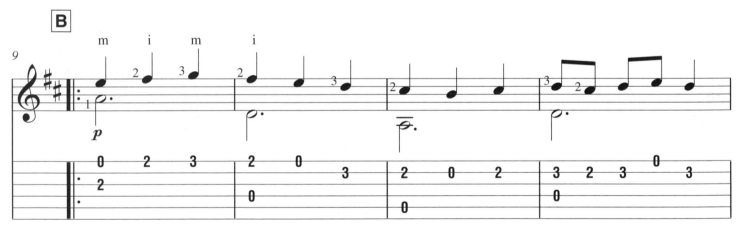

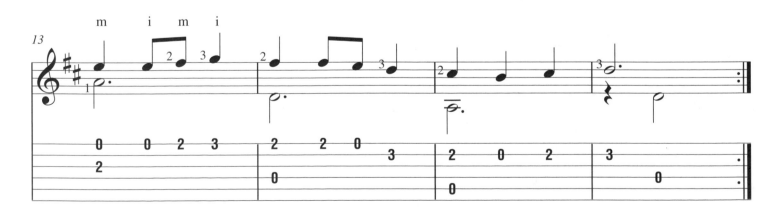

Scarborough Fair

Traditional English

Moderato

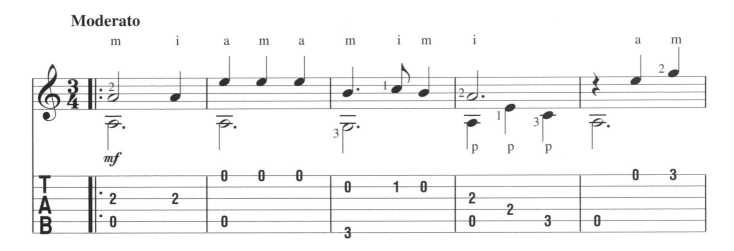

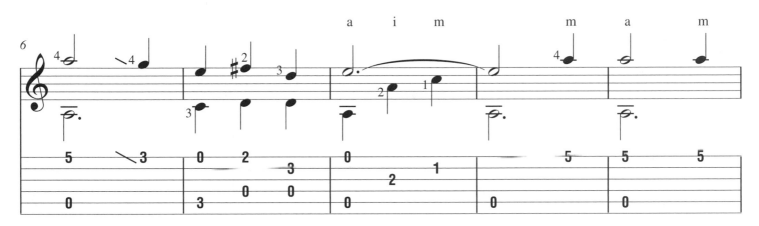

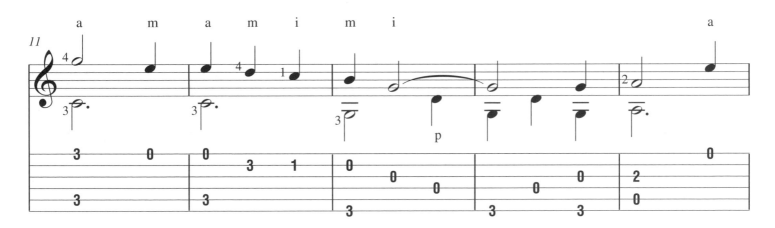

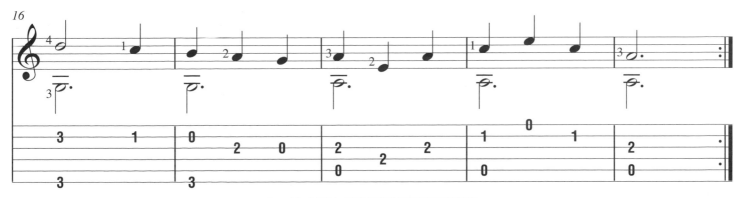

Allegretto

Fernando Sor
(c. 1778-1839)

Moderato

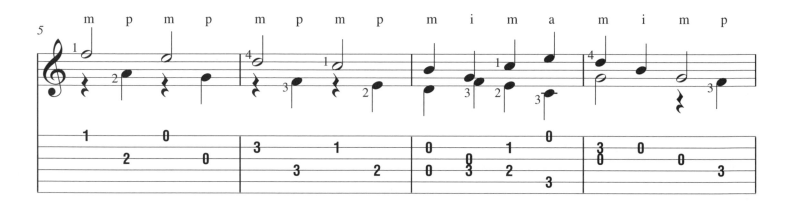

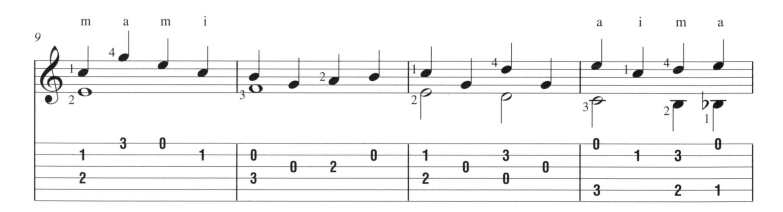

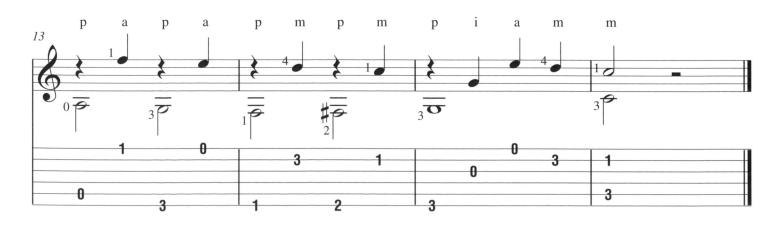

Wee Cooper O'Fife

Irish Folk Song

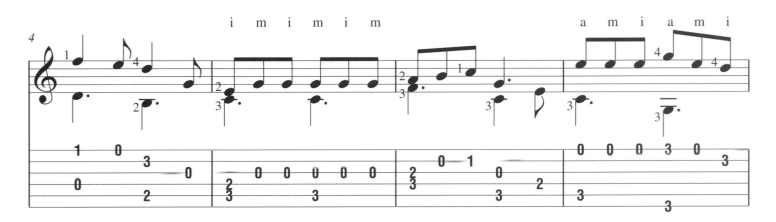

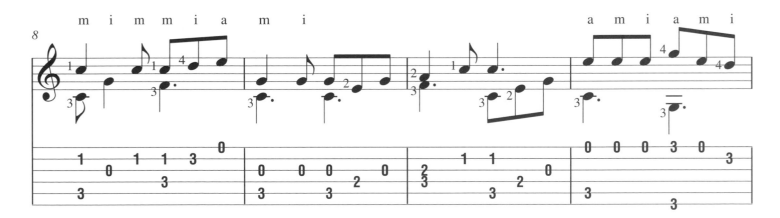

Simple Gifts

Shaker Song
Joseph Brackett
(1797-1882)

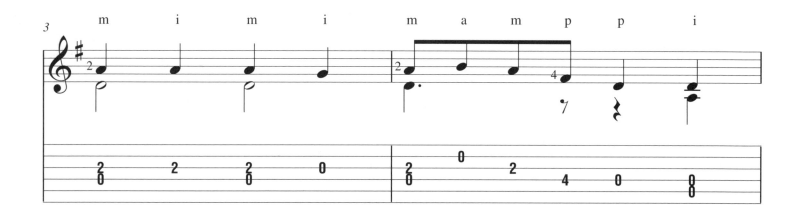

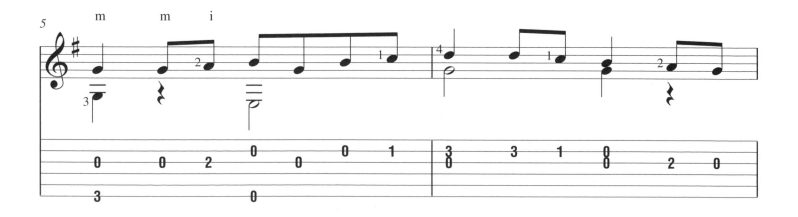

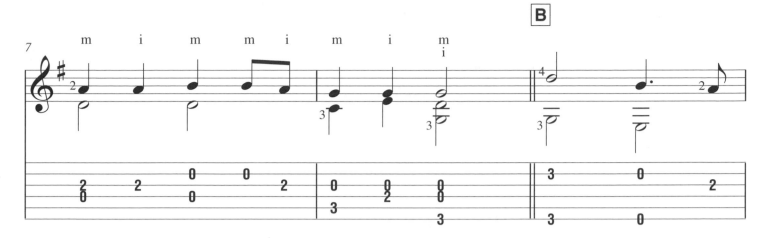

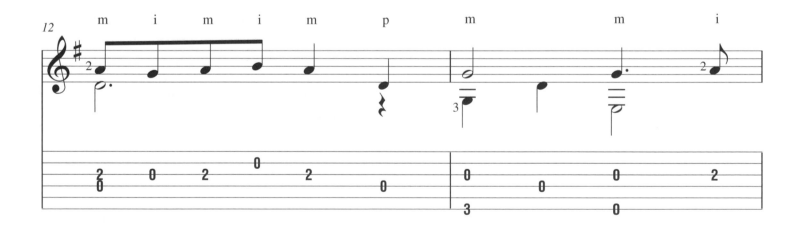

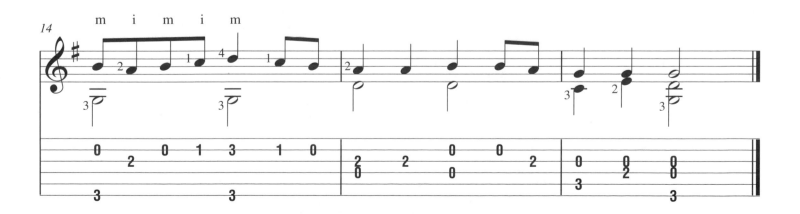

The Ash Grove

Welsh Folk Song
(c.1800)

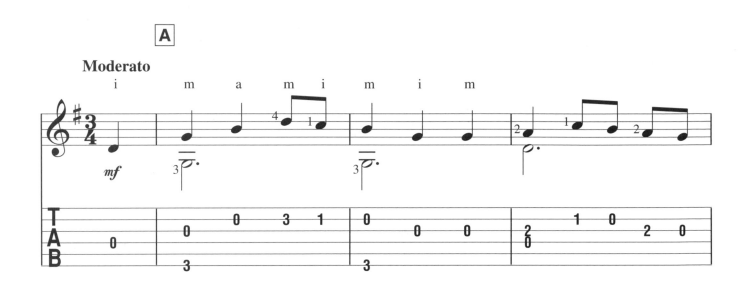

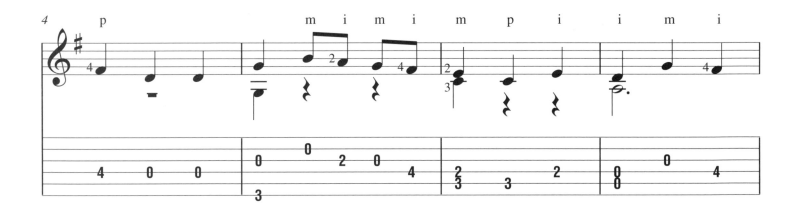

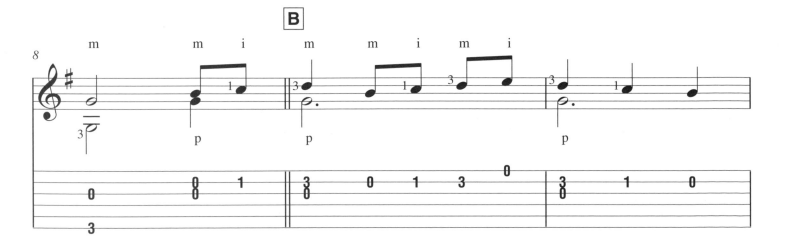

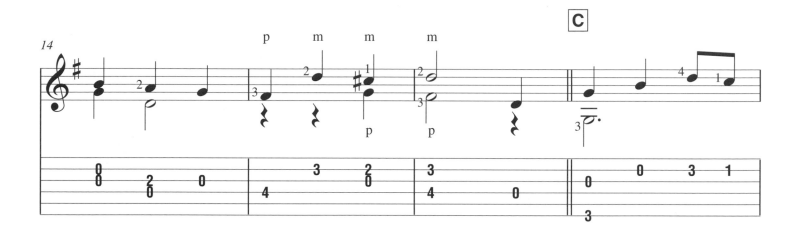

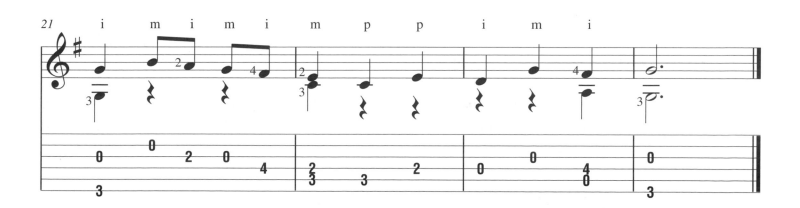

Study in A Minor

Dionisio Aguado
(1784-1849)

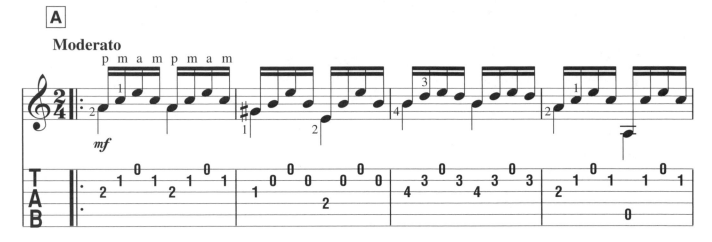

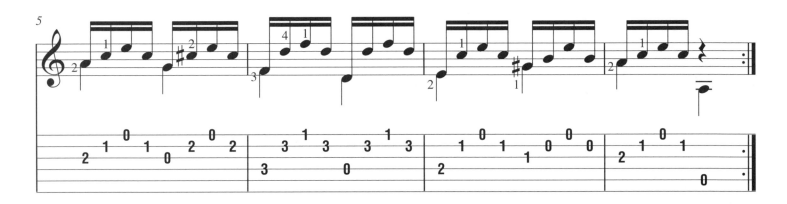

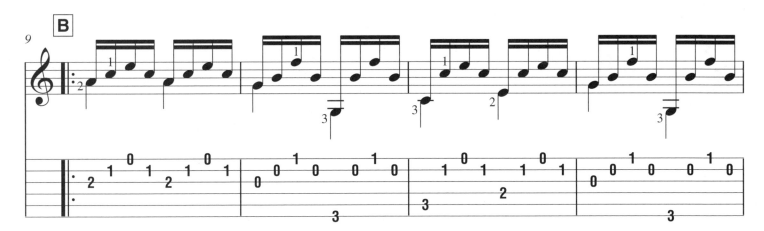

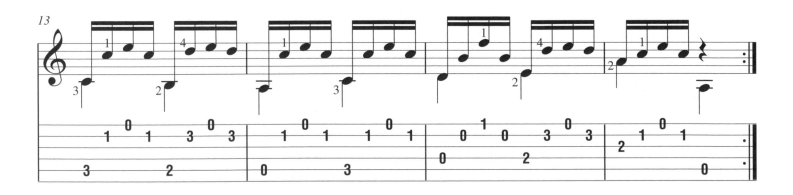

Study in C Major

Dionisio Aguado
(1784-1849)

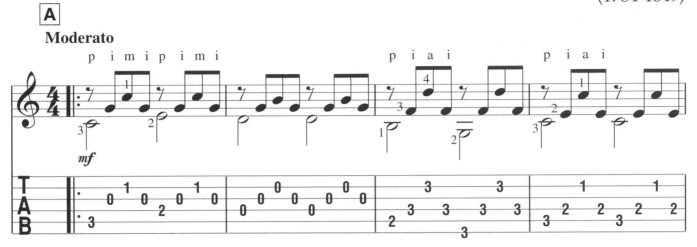

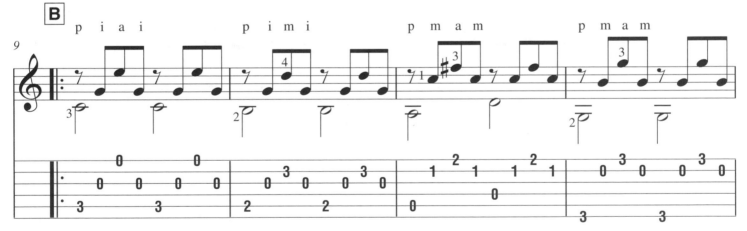

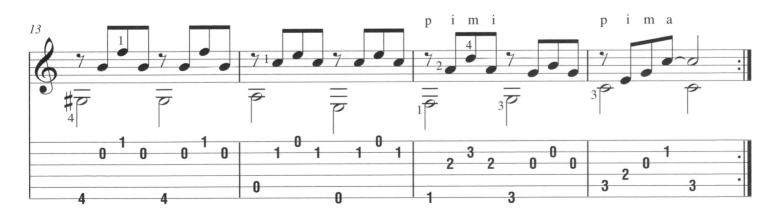

Prelude No. 1, Op. 114

Ferdinando Carulli
(1770-1841)

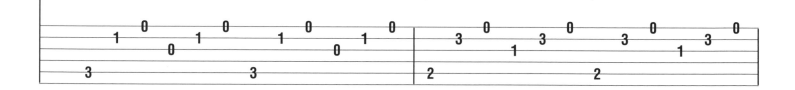

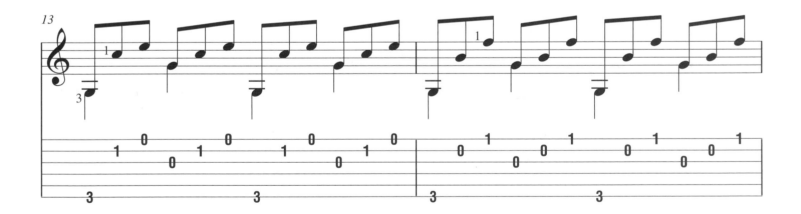

Prelude No. 2, Op. 114

Ferdinando Carulli
(1770-1841)

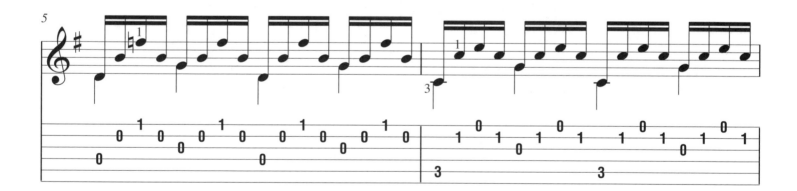

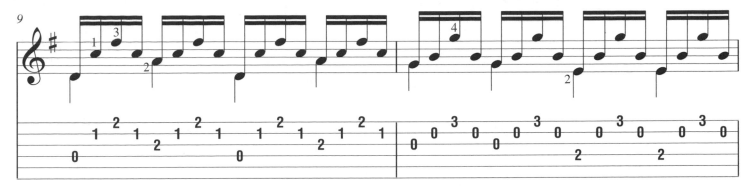

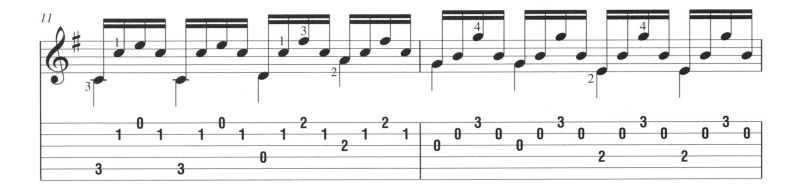

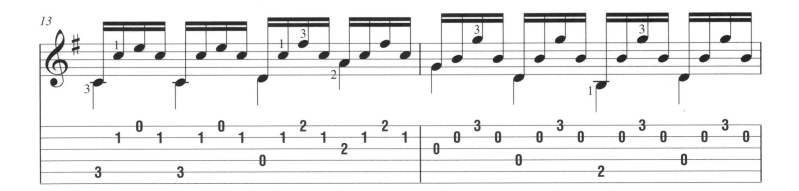

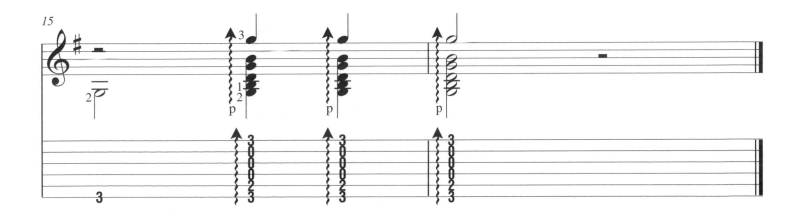

Prelude No. 3, Op. 114

Ferdinando Carulli
(1770-1841)

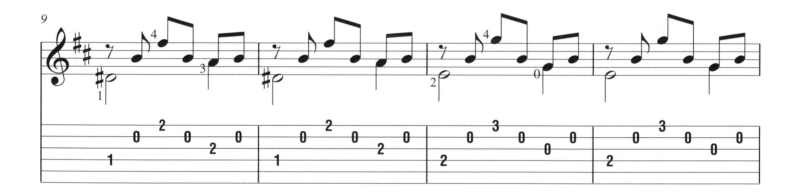

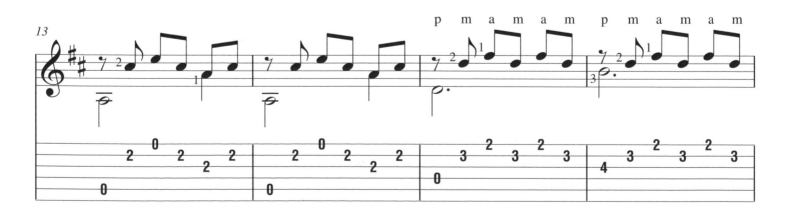

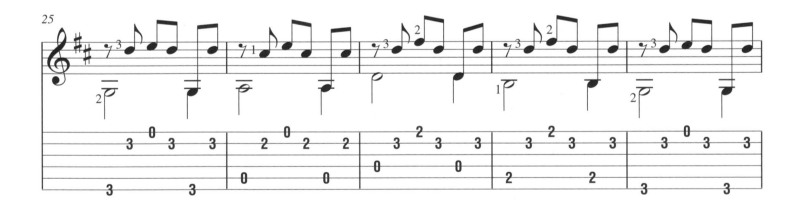

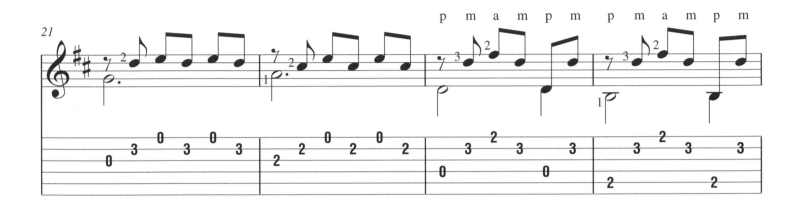

Malagueña

Traditional Spanish

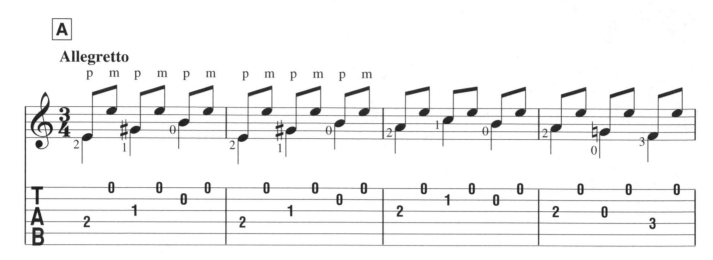

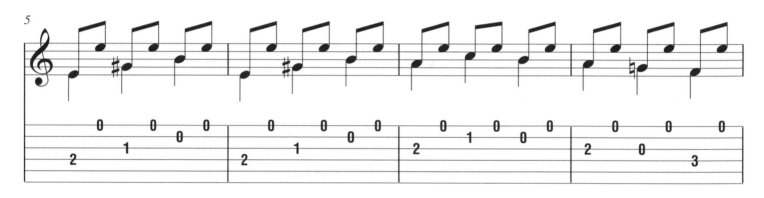

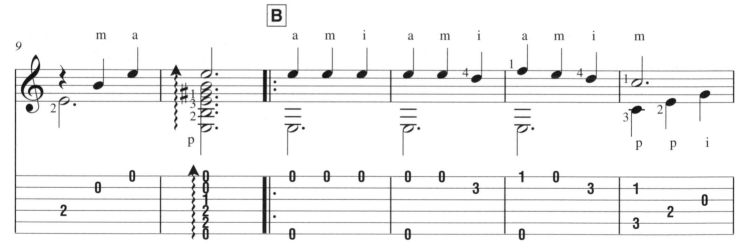

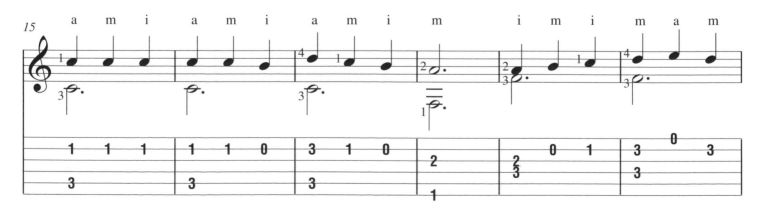

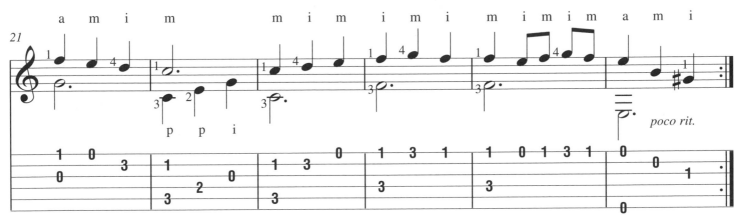

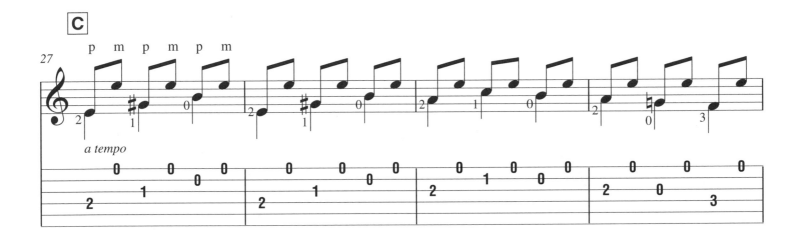

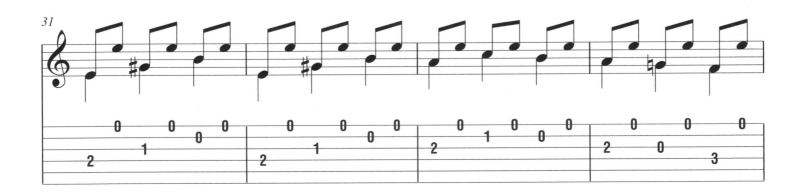

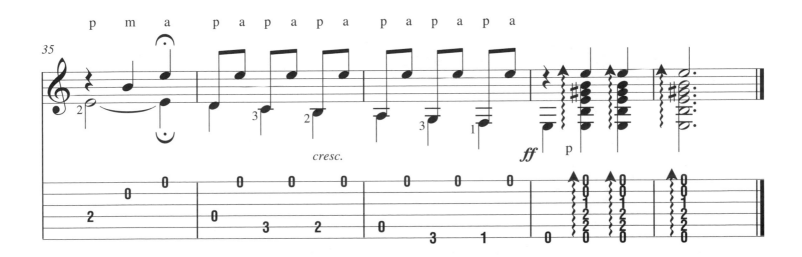

Allegretto

Ferdinando Carulli
(1770-1841)

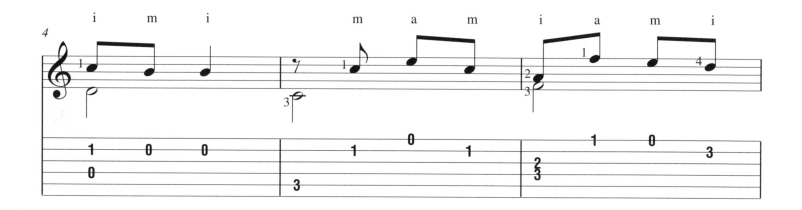

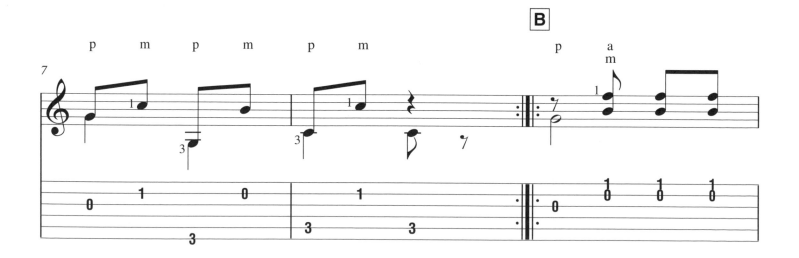

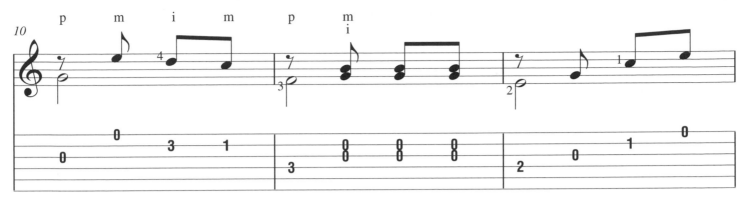

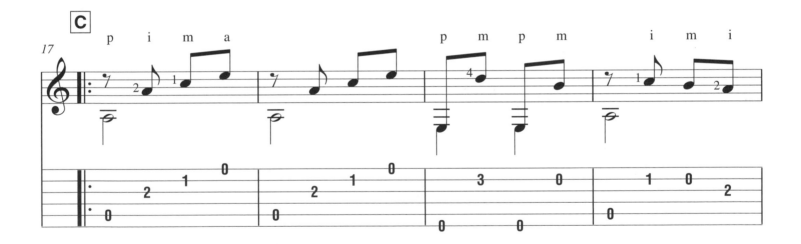

Country Dance

Ferdinando Carulli
(1770-1841)

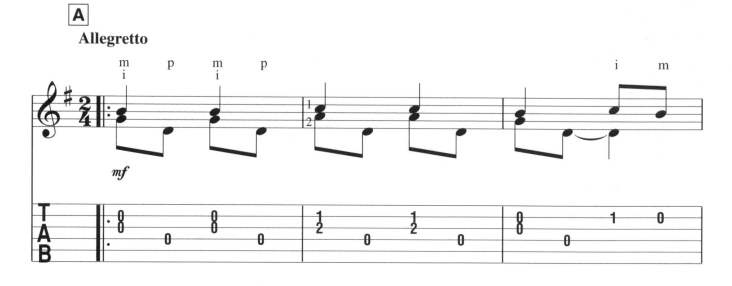

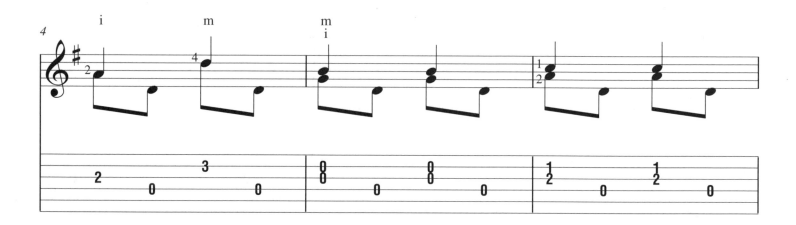

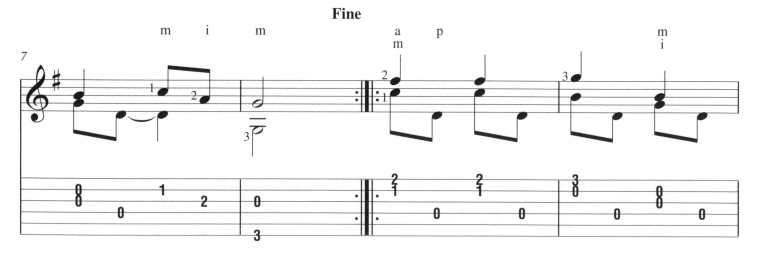

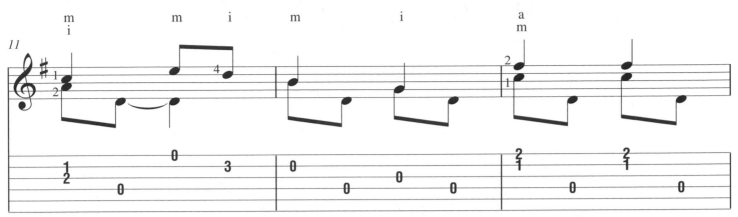

D.C. al Fine

34

Waltz No. 1, Op. 121

Ferdinando Carulli
(1770-1841)

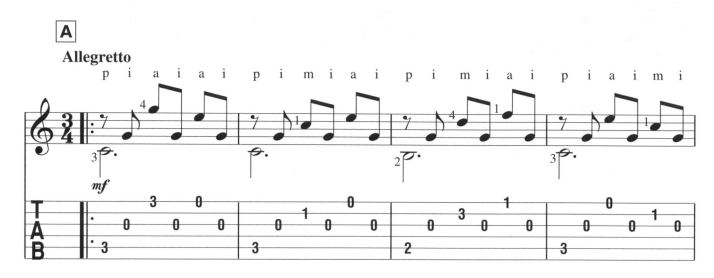

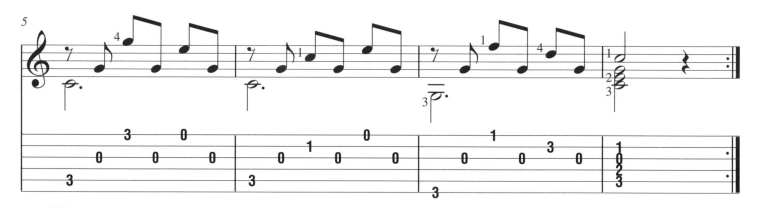

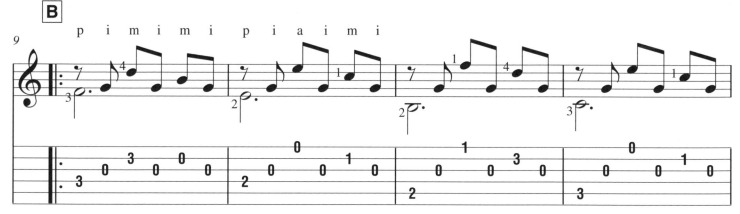

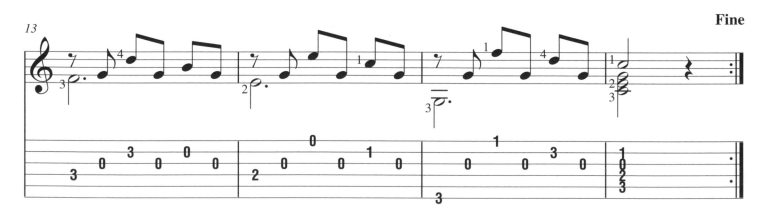

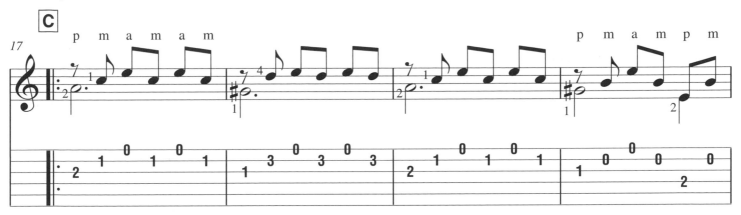

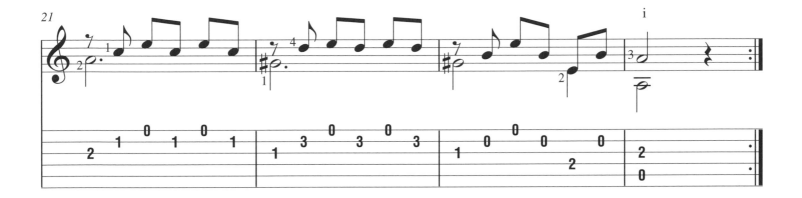

D.C. al Fine

Amazing Grace

Spiritual

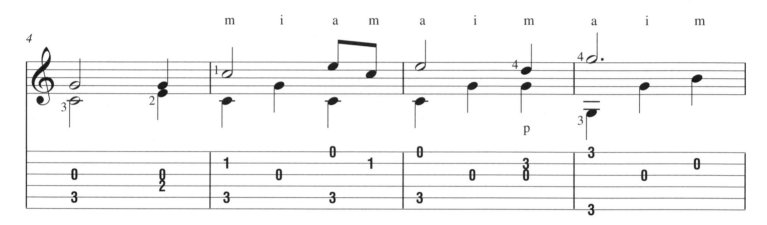

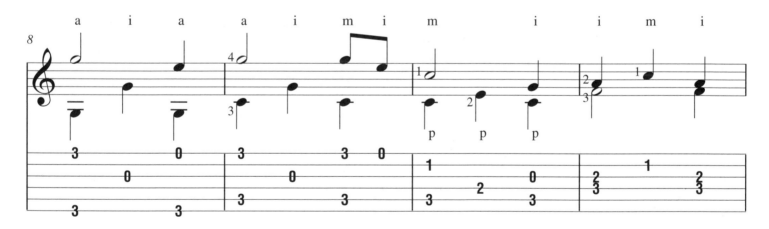

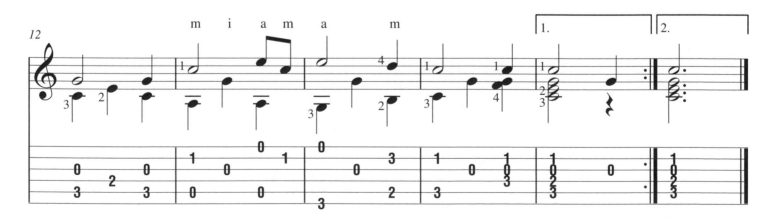

Ode to Joy

Ludwig van Beethoven
(1770-1827)

Ecossaise No. 2, Op. 33

Mauro Giuliani
(1781-1829)

Ecossaise No. 10, Op. 33

Mauro Giuliani
(1781-1829)

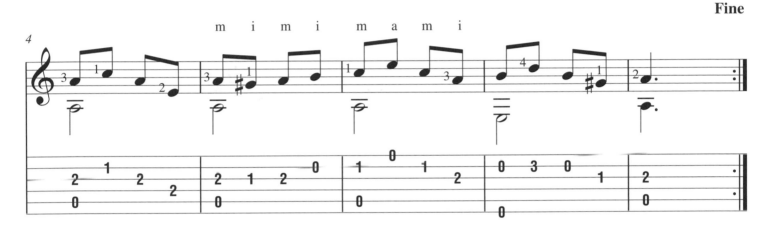

English Dance

Ferdinando Carulli
(1770-1841)

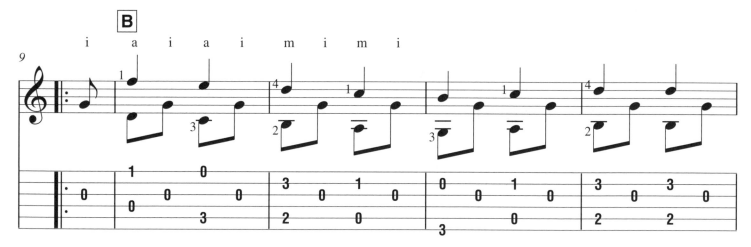

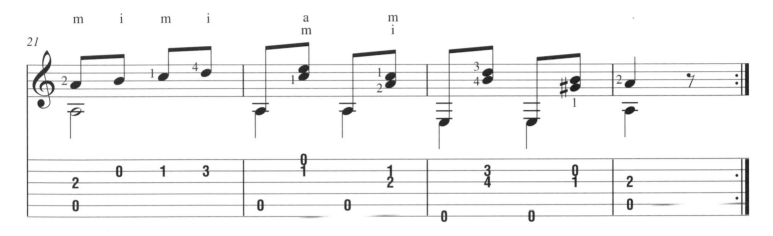

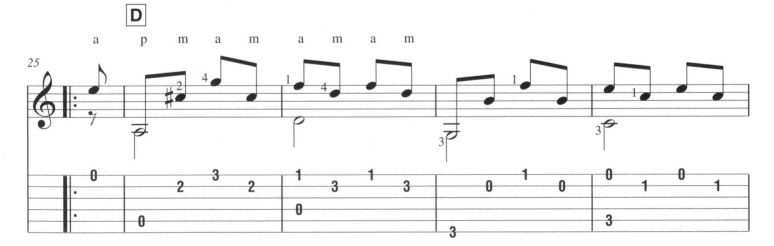

D.C. al Fine

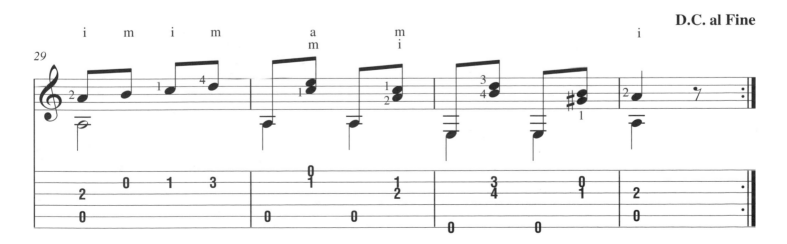

Shenandoah

Folk Song

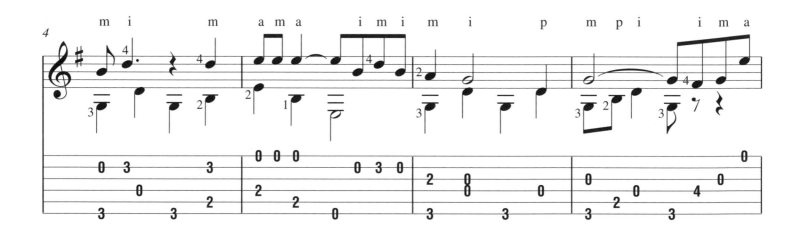

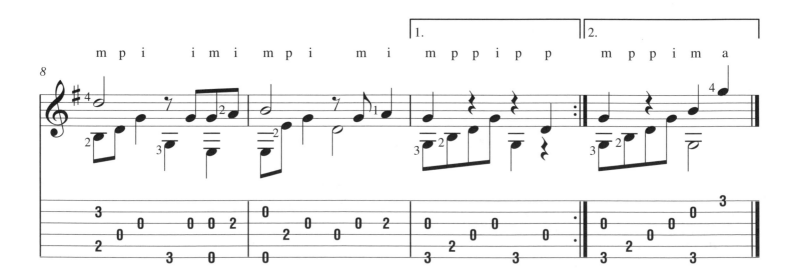

Calleno Costure Me

Anonymous
16th c.

A

Moderato

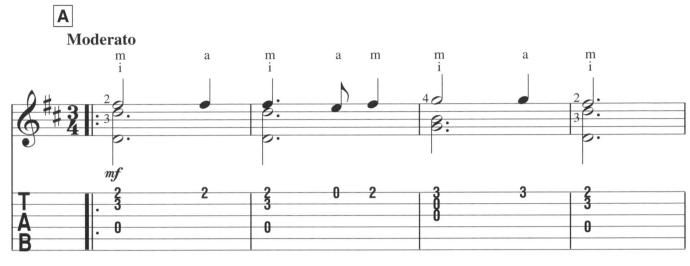

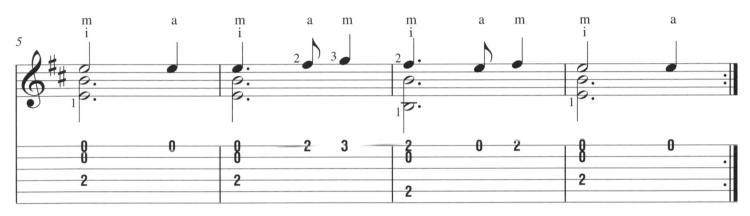

B

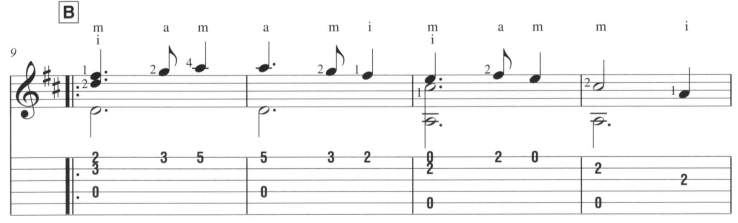

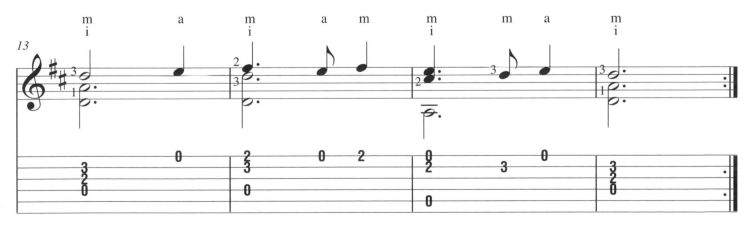

Menuett

Johann Philipp Krieger
(1649-1725)

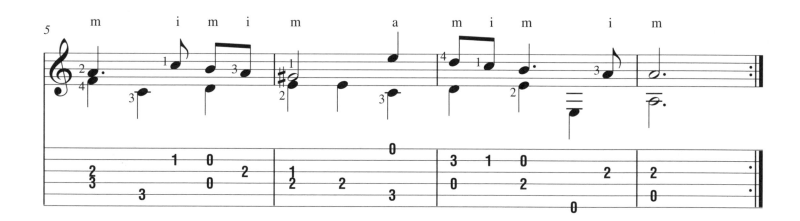

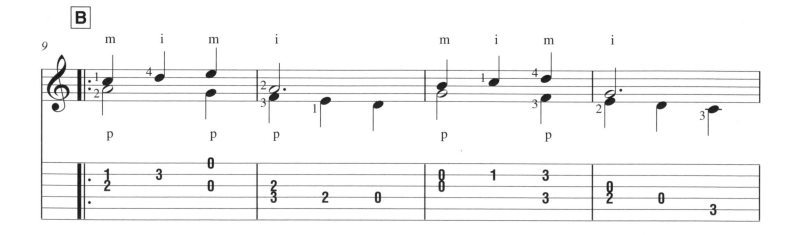

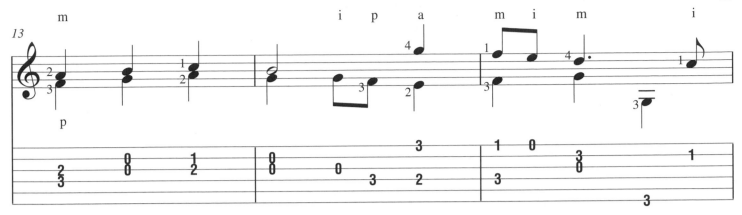

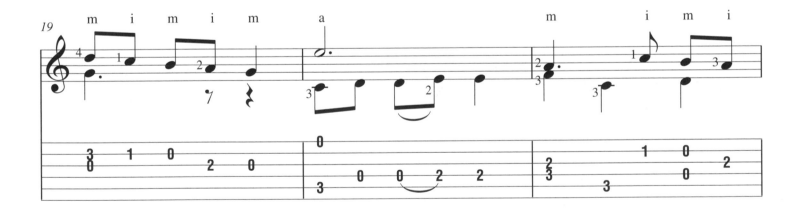

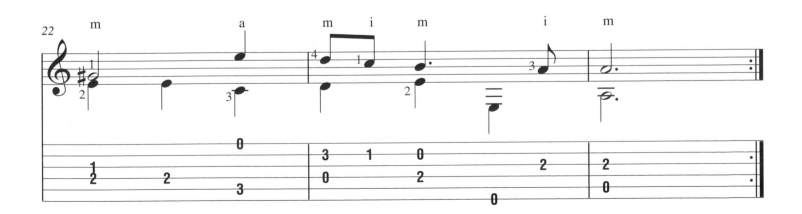

Españoleto

Gaspar Sanz
(1640-1710)

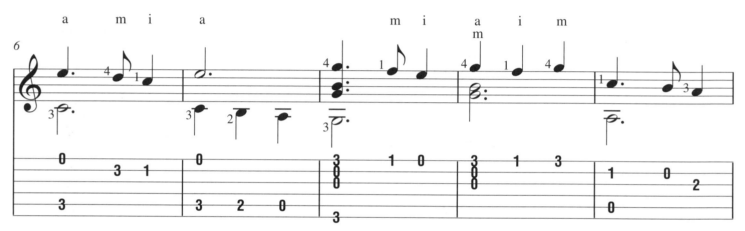

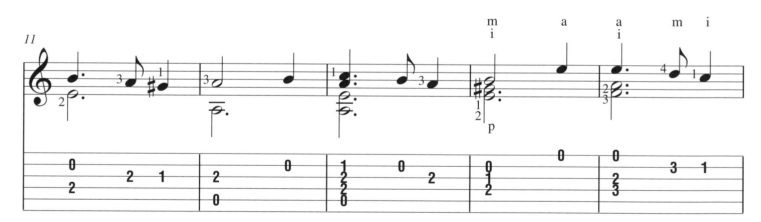

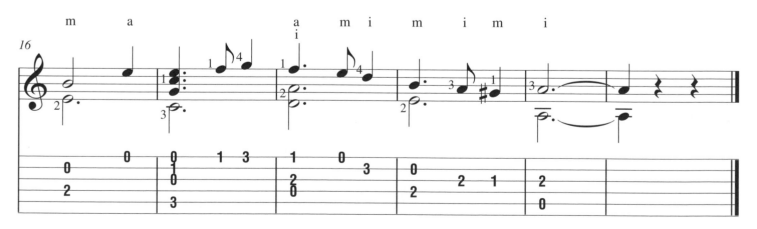

Greensleeves

Anonymous
English 16th c.

The Minstrel Boy

Traditional Irish

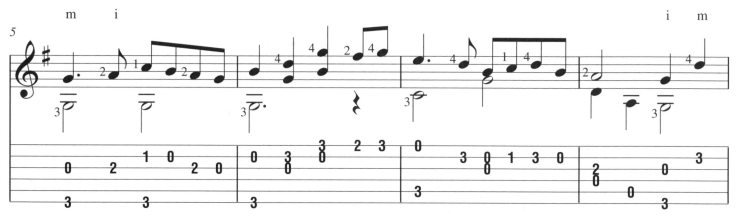